THE
GOLDEN AGE
OF
VILLAGE CRICKET

THE GOLDEN AGE OF VILLAGE CRICKET

STEVEN GARNER

FOREWORD BY

BRIAN JOHNSTON

Lennard Publishing
1988

*For my wife, Nicky, who was the
inspiration behind this book.*

LENNARD PUBLISHING
a division of Lennard Books Ltd
92 Hastings Street
Luton, Beds LU1 5BH

Garner, Steven
　The golden age of village cricket.
　1. English humorous cartoons – Collections
　from individual artists
　I. Title
　741.5'942

ISBN 1 85291 036 4

First published 1988
Copyright © Steven Garner 1988

Cover design by Pocknell & Co
Typesetting by Nuprint Ltd
Printed and bound in Great Britain by The Bath Press

FOREWORD

BY

BRIAN JOHNSTON

I am lucky to have a marvellous job as a cricket commentator. In 42 summers I have covered just under 250 Tests, and I have enjoyed every minute of it. But my first love is still village cricket. John Arlott's voice with its Hampshire burr used to conjure up a smell of bat oil and new mown grass, and a picture of white figures on a village green. In the background would be the parish church and of course the local pub as the headquarters of the village side. That to me is where real cricket is still played and Steven Garner's cartoons bring it all to life 'before your very eyes', as Arthur Askey used to say.

I played for my village as a boy, and I still stop to watch a village game when motoring around the country. Of course things have changed with the times but the basic spirit of cricket is still there. No longer do the squire and the vicar get automatically chosen. The village blacksmith, when there is one, no longer wears braces and black trousers as he hurls his bouncers at the batsman. Television has had a big influence. Fielders now field close in at short-leg, though thankfully not yet in helmets. The wicketkeeper no longer has a longstop. The outfield is no longer a crop of hay with hidden cowpats. The ground is now beautifully kept, usually mowed and rolled by willing volunteers from the local team.

There are still plenty of local Derbies and friendlies, and now there is also the extra rivalry and competition of the Village Championship, with the two finalists battling it out at Lords' at the end of August. But some things never change and thank goodness the ladies, God bless them, still cut the sandwiches and make the cakes for the main event of the afternoon—the tea.

Of course we must not forget the umpires. Most villages still have what they normally call 'our umpire'. They too have benefitted from television and no longer justify the sort of stories which used to be told about them. There was, for instance, the home umpire who gave one of 'his' batsmen not out when the ball hit him on the knee right in front of the stumps.

'Why wasn't he out?' asked the bowler.

'Too high,' replied the umpire.

The next ball hit the batsman on his boot, again right in front of the stumps.

'Hows that?'
'Not out.'
'Why not, this time?'
'Too low.'

Equipment is much better these days. The village side always used to share bats and pads which were kept in one old bag. Nowadays most players have their own. Once many years ago a batsman came in with only one pad and that was on his right leg. One of the fielders pointed this out to him.

'Yes. I know. We've only got three pads between us.'
'But you have got it on the wrong leg.'
'Oh, no I haven't. I thought I would be batting at the other end.'

Finally, as I've said, the vicar used to be an automatic choice. A young curate was once bowling against a bishop who was playing for the visiting team. He thought he would be kind and get him off the mark with a slow full-pitch. The bishop promptly hit it out of the ground.

'I'm sorry, young man,' said the bishop, 'I've hit you right out of your parish.'

This annoyed the curate who went back to his mark, rushed up and bowled a vicious bouncer which hit the bishop in his midriff. He collapsed on the ground in agony.

'I'm sorry, m'lord,' said the curate, 'I seem to have hit you in the middle of your diocese.'

So there you are. So long as there's village cricket there will always be fun. I hope that Steven Garner will continue to portray it for us in his delightful way.

Brian Johnston

A PRE-MATCH INSPECTION OF THE WICKET BY TH

PPOSITION AT MOUNT CHAPPEL, COUNTY DURHAM

MEMBERS OF THE PIGHTLEFORD TEAM TRAVELLING TO
AN AWAY MATCH, 1896

GEORGE CLUMP, GROUNDSMAN AT EARLS PICKTON, SUSSEX,
PREPARING HIS WICKET

AN EARLY COWPAT SCOOPER AT HERONSTALL, GLOUCESTERSHIRE,
CIRCA 1900

THE PLAYERS FROM LAKELY HEATH, NORFOLK, WATCHING WITH ANXIETY
TO SEE IF GOLDINGSFIELD HAVE TURNED UP WITH THEIR NOTORIOUS FAST BOWLER

FRANK TOLLOCKSTON, GROUNDSMAN AT BRINTHAM-IN-THE-VALE, HEREFORDSHIRE, WITH THE CLUB'S MOWER

THE CHANGING FACILITIES AT LINGFORD BRAY, OXFORDSHIRE, 1900

ALBERT QUICKSAW IN HIS GARDEN AT SIMPLY TRUSSCOTT, CORNWALL, WHERE
HE WOULD ALWAYS LIGHT A BONFIRE AT 2.30 ON A SATURDAY AFTERNOON

MEMBERS OF THE DITCHWORTH COMMON TEAM ATTEMPTING TO
PUT IN THE STUMPS DURING THE LONG HOT SUMMER OF 1900

CHARLIE BRINDED, CAPTAIN OF FAGGOTTS GREEN, SUSSEX, FEEDING
HIS OPENING BOWLER BEFORE A MATCH, CIRCA 1890

TRYING TO LOCATE THE GROUND AT GREAT CHADBURY, ESSEX

CHILDREN EMPLOYED TO PICK UP STONES FROM THE WICKET PRIOR TO
THE MATCH AT BREWIS TAYFIELD, LINCOLNSHIRE, 1898

MARKING THE BOUNDARY AT BEAUCHAMP CROSS, NORTHAMPTONSHIRE

THE CHANGING ROOM AT MUCKLE END, WORCESTERSHIRE, 1909

OPTIMISTIC CAPTAINS AT CRABBS GREEN, SURREY

LOOKING FOR THE BALL AT PARRACKSFIEL

WALTER SPROT OF TINKLES CROSS, NORTHAMPTONSHIRE, REMOVING LAST SEASON'S
MUD PRIOR TO THE FIRST MATCH OF 1897

THE ANNUAL BOXING DAY MATCH AT RIGGISTONE, YORKSHIRE, 1894

TAKING A REFRESHMENT BREAK AT THATCHBURY, BUCKINGHAMSHIRE, ON
A COLD APRIL SATURDAY IN 1901

FOUR PLAYERS FROM PLUMBRIDGE, GLOUCESTERSHIRE, FIND RELIEF WITH
THE FALL OF THE FIRST WICKET AFTER LUNCH

**A SUDDEN CHANGE OF TEMPERATURE
AT CASTLE PATTERSWICK, NORTHUMBERLAND, 1896**

A PLAYER FROM PARSLEYCOMBE, WARWICKSHIRE, CHASING A WIDE DELIVERY

BOWLING INTO THE WIND AT WELLOW-ON-THE-HILL, AFTER THE
UMPIRES HAD AGREED TO PLAY WITHOUT STUMPS

'RUTHLESS' REG BUCKET CLAIMING ANOTHER VICTIM,
AT MUCH BAMBERRY, HAMPSHIRE, 1908

**ALBERT BRINKLEY OF EAST SHODDINGHAM, STAFFORDSHIRE,
ON HIS WEDDING DAY, 1908**

MAJOR A. J. T. BRAND-SPILLINGHAM BATTING
IN A LIGHT DRIZZLE AT ROSSLEY MANOR, 1892

**AN UNKNOWN PLAYER FROM LIDDLE, STAFFORDSHIRE, GIVING VENT TO HIS
FEELINGS AFTER FAILING TO TROUBLE THE SCORERS**

HERBERT MEAD WATCHING A MATCH FROM HIS GARDEN GATE
AT PARSONS HOLEGATE, HAMPSHIRE, CIRCA 1895

JOE RIST OF SCAPFORD, NOTTINGHAMSHIRE, BEING INFORMED
BY HIS SKIPPER THAT IT IS HIS TURN TO BAT

THE VILLAGE GROUND AT GRINDON,
WHERE A PUBLIC FOOTPATH CROSSES THE PITCH

THE FIRST FLYING MACHINE TO PASS OVE

LUCKLEY HALL, BERKSHIRE, 1911

MISS EMILY HOLLINGSWORTH
AT HER VERY FIRST CRICKET MATCH, LYNNBURY, STAFFORDSHIRE

PERCY THEAKSTONE TREATING A BOUNCER WITH INDIFFERENCE AFTER AN ENJOYABLE LUNCH IN THE THREE FERRETS, TUPTON SMEALEY, OXFORDSHIRE, 1906

A PLAYER FROM WELKSFORD, CHESHIRE, BEING GIVEN A STERN LECTURE BY MR TIBBINS,
THE SCORER, HAVING HAD THE AUDACITY TO LOOK AT THE SCOREBOOK DURING THE GAME

GEORGE PLACEFENDER OF CAMPION END, WARWICKSHIRE, PLAYING HIS
SURPRISINGLY SUCCESSFUL 'BACKING-AWAY-TO-SQUARE-LEG' SHOT

JACK 'FERRET' BREWSTER OF MAGGOTS END, HERTFORDSHIRE, WHO CLAIMED TO BE AN OFF-BREAK
BOWLER, ALTHOUGH, THROUGHOUT HIS LONG CAREER, HE WAS NEVER KNOWN TO TURN THE BALL

THE CAPTAIN OF BEACHWOOD END, WARWICKSHIRE, LISTENING TO ADVICE FROM SPECTATORS ON THE BOUNDARY, CIRCA 1899

ALOYSIUS 'GLOVES' CAMPBELL, WHO IN 27 YEARS AS WICKETKEEPER
FOR PIGSEAROLE GREEN, ESSEX, NEVER ONCE TOOK THE BALL CLEANLY

**A PLAYER FROM LONG PYFORD, CAMBRIDGESHIRE,
BEING BEATEN IN THE FLIGHT**

DICK 'STAG' BALDWIN,
THE UMPIRE FOR FORD GREEN, WILTSHIRE, 1904

SYD FERRIS FROM STOKEBECK, LANCASHIRE, PREPARING TO BAT, 1893

BILL RUTTER FIELDING THE BALL WITH HIS TRUSTY RIGHT FOOT
AT WEEDON PITCHCUTT, BEDFORDSHIRE, CIRCA 1893

FRED PRATT OF FLITCHTHORPE, SUSSEX, AFTER BEING
GIVEN OUT LBW, FIRST BALL

THE SIGHTSCREEN AT GREAT ASHSTOCK, CIRCA 1910

THE UMPIRE AT GOATLEY GREEN, LEICESTERSHIRE

S DEBUT FOR TYE, SUFFOLK, 1900

THE SLOPING OUTFIELD AT GREAT WELTING, DERBYSHIRE, 1909

A FIELDER AT CAMOMILE GREEN REFUSING TO CONCEDE A BOUNDARY

BATTING ON A STICKY WICKET AT ARLBURY, LINCOLNSHIRE, 1914

GEORGE SCUTTLE, THE EMINENT PIPE-SMOKING UMPIRE
FROM WOODHAM SCRAPHEDGE, NORFOLK

PLAYERS FROM WIDLEY, SUSSEX, ABOUT TO ENTER THE TOILETS

A DROPPED CATCH AT THORNTON-IN-THE-CLAY, DERBYSHIRE, 1912

CHARLES 'GRINDER' LITTLE, THE OPENING BATSMAN FOR HIGH CAXTED, 1901

**HORACE TWIGG RETRIEVING THE BALL FROM
THE VILLAGE POND AT STIMPTON PLIDWICK, 1905**

HARRY EDGEWORTH, THE INFAMOUS DORSET UMPIRE,
TURNS DOWN ANOTHER APPEAL

BETWEEN INNINGS AT SMEW, 1910,
WHERE THE TEA WAS THE TALK OF THE WHOLE OF DEVON

**THE LIGHT ROLLER BEING USED AT CHEASLEY COMMON,
YORKSHIRE, 1899**

A PLAYER AT MUSHBURY-ON-THE-GREEN, WARWICKSHIRE, ATTEMPTING TO
LEAVE THE TABLE WITHOUT FINISHING ONE OF MRS SCROGGLEY'S HOME-MADE APPLE PIES

SCRANTON BROADASH, THE FIRST VILLAGE CLUB
IN RUTLAND TO INSTALL WASHING FACILITIES

THE CAPTAIN OF SPARROW END
LOOKING FOR A VOLUNTEER TO UMPIRE

TAKING TEA AT HAWKRIDG

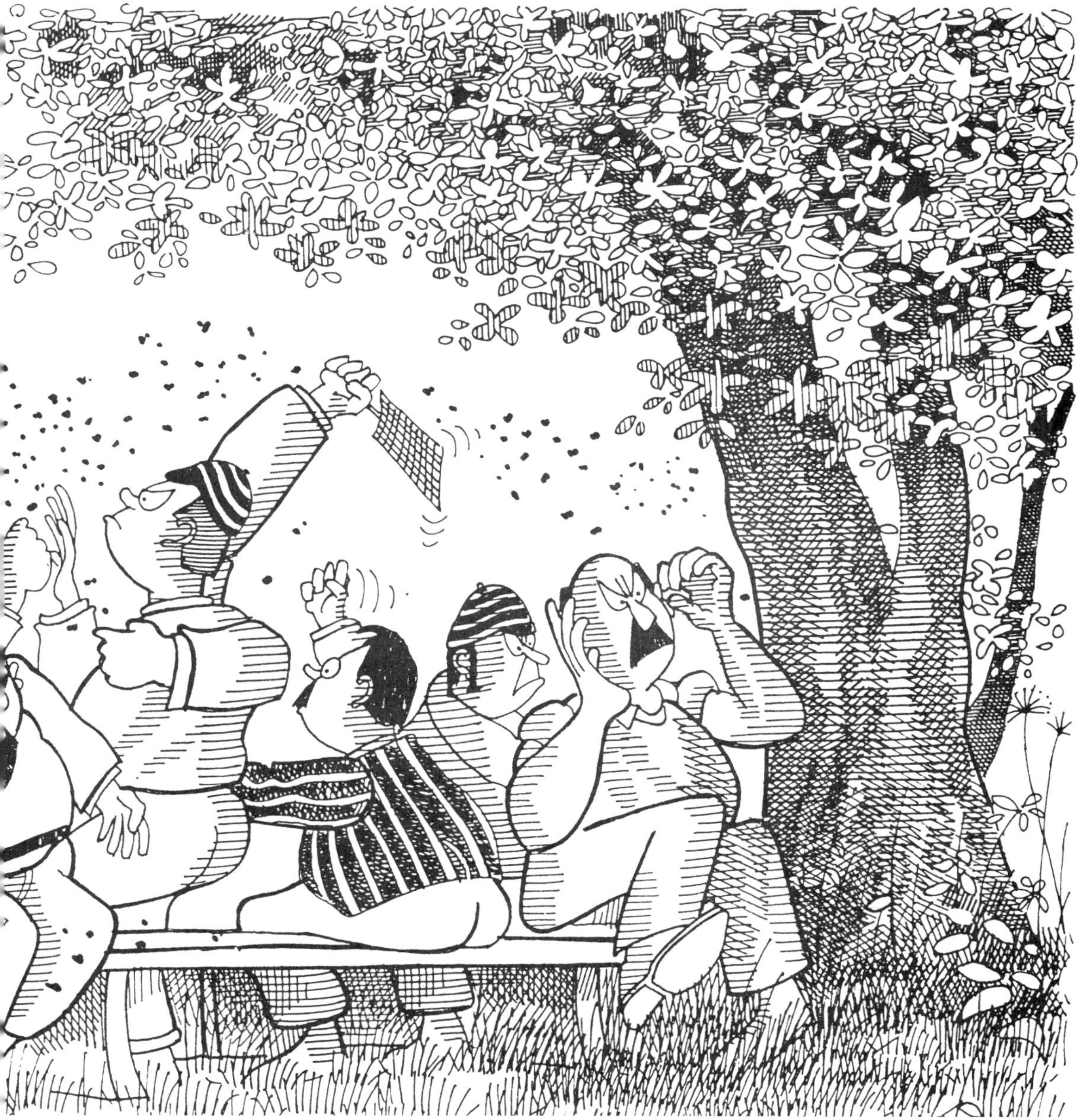

MERSET, 1896

BATTING AT MOLDWICK, SUFFOLK, AFTER ONE OF
THE WETTEST MAYS SINCE RECORDS BEGAN

**ALBERT GRUTT, OPENING BOWLER FOR MOUSLEY GREEN,
GLOUCESTERSHIRE, BEGINNING HIS APPROACH**

WALTER HAGGER OF LONG WARPSBURY, BEDFORDSHIRE,
WHO ALWAYS STOOD UP TO EVERY BOWLER

BATTING AT STAGGERTON AMPWICK, WITH ITS FAMOUS OAK TREE

THE REVEREND CHARLES FURNINGHAM OF PLESHFORD, 1912

CYRIL HARE OF MOLESCOMBE, DEVON, RETIRING HURT
AFTER BATTING WITHOUT A BOX, 1897

**HARRY HAWKER, THE VILLAGE POACHER
OF FROXLEY UPPER GREEN, GLOUCESTERSHIRE, 1902**

A SLIP CATCH GOES BEGGING AT PINDLEWICK, CUMBERLAND, 1900

**BILL LONGSTAFF OF BENTONS MEAD, BUCKINGHAMSHIRE, PLAYING WITH
THE SAME BAT THAT HE FIRST USED AS A 15 YEAR OLD**

**THE WICKET AT HACKERS STREET, STAFFORDSHIRE,
WHICH HAD A REPUTATION FOR BEING DANGEROUS**

**THE UMPIRE FROM EAST COWSHILL, SOMERSET,
IS ASKED HIS OPINION BY ALBERT EVANS, CIRCA 1897**

THE CAPTAIN OF GLIMPFORD TRYING TO DECIDE JUST
WHERE TO HIDE THE PRINGLE BROTHERS

ACTION FROM THE MATCH BETWEEN LOCAL RIVALS,
GREAT BABBAGE AND LITTLE BABBAGE, 1904

THE GROUND AT CLUTTERFORD END, WORCESTERSHIRE, WHICH WAS KNOWN AS
ONE OF THE MOST PICTURESQUE IN THE COUNTY, CIRCA 1900

A MATCH IN PROGRESS

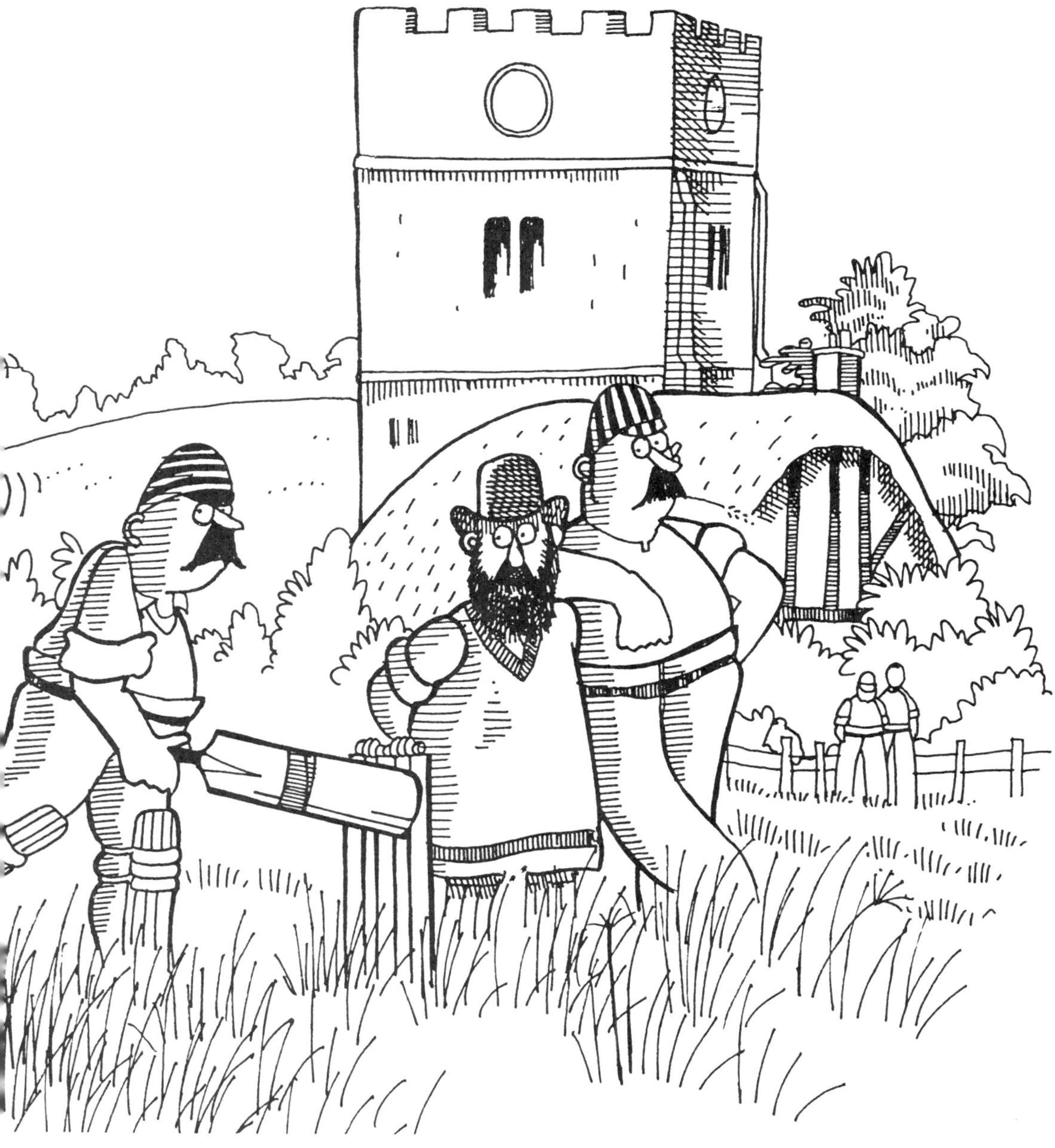

DLERS GREEN, HAMPSHIRE

SYD GREYGOOSE, OPENING BOWLER FOR UPPER DENZIL,
NOTTINGHAMSHIRE, 1913

**GENERAL A. R. G. 'TEDDY' GROAT-FURNESS
OF TRUNDLE, KENT, PREPARING TO BAT, 1905**

GEORGE 'NUTTY' WOOD OF TRIMPLEY, LEICESTERSHIRE. HIS PERSISTENT GRIN AND
IRRITATING HABITS MADE HIM ONE OF THE MOST UNPOPULAR PLAYERS IN THE AREA

FIELDERS AT SHICKLE GREEN ATTEMPTING TO RETRIEVE THE BALL
FROM AN ADJACENT FIELD, 1902

EDWARD MINNS ATTEMPTING TO OBSTRUCT THE BOWLER
AT MUFFINGTON, WILTSHIRE, 1911

THE WICKET AT PUXTED GREEN, OXFORDSHIRE, 1897

ARTHUR 'TRIGGER' CROW OF SANDCOCKS END, KENT. HE WAS
ACKNOWLEDGED TO HAVE THE FASTEST FINGER IN THE WHOLE OF THE SOUTH-EAST

PERCY BRISLEY OF LONG HEDGING, WILTSHIRE (LEFT),
WHO ALWAYS PLAYED WITH HIS WALLET IN HIS BACK POCKET

CHARLIE PEBBLE, WHO WOULD RARELY ATTEMPT TO PLAY THE BALL
WITH HIS BAT, IN ACTION AT SUTTON JOWERS, LANCASHIRE

F. D. M. PARTRIDGE OF EAST GRINGLEY, KENT,
THE CELEBRATED ROUND-ARM BOWLER

A PLAYER RETIRING HURT AT GREAT WATHAM,
ESSEX, AFTER FALLING DOWN A RABBIT HOLE, 1911

**BARTHOLOMEW HAYDEN, THE NOTORIOUSLY TALKATIVE WICKETKEEPER
FROM HIGH RUDING, ESSEX**

**NEVILLE BUCKLE FROM PEARS GREEN, KENT,
APPEALING FOR A CATCH AT THE WICKET**

**MARCUS PETHERICK FIELDING ON THE BOUNDARY AT FIVE OAK GREEN,
AFTER NOT BEING ALLOWED TO OPEN THE BOWLING**

HARRY HIGGS, THE VILLAGE MOLE CATCHER
OF BRAMPTON SNERDLOCK, 1907

THE REVEREND H. J. PALFREY AND WIFE PASSING THE PAVILION
AT WIDDINGTREE, WILTSHIRE, 1902

ARTHUR 'PINKY' RADWINTER THE FAMOUS LEG-BREAK
AND GOOGLY BOWLER FROM POLLOCKS DOWN, SUSSEX

SYD CALDERCOTT OF LITTLE FENNY, SUSSEX, PLAYING THE
ONLY SHOT IN HIS REPERTOIRE

**FRED 'SLOGGER' DIGSLEY OF SOMERTON GREEN
COMPLAINS OF INTIMIDATION**

BATTING AT STOCK-IN-THE-WATER, DERBYSHIRE, WHERE THE SOFT WICKET
WAS REGARDED AS ONE OF THE SLOWEST AND LOWEST IN THE COUNTY

IN THE LOCAL DERBY BETWEEN GREAT DUNGBURY AND LITTLE DUNGBURY
IT WAS NOT UNCOMMON FOR ONE SIDE TO TRY TO GAIN AN UNFAIR ADVANTAGE

GEORGE ALLENBY, PROPRIETOR OF ALLENBY'S SPORTS SHOP, SIGNING UP
A NEW CUSTOMER AT PINNOCKS END, HERTFORDSHIRE

ISAIAH SPROAT, WHO WAS STILL PLAYING IN HIS NINETIES
FOR SGRAGGSWAITE, YORKSHIRE

CHARLES HERRINGSHAW, THE SQUIRE'S SON FROM YIPTON,
WORCESTERSHIRE, TAKING A CATCH ON THE BOUNDARY

A SUNDAY EVENING DISTURBANCE AT MUNWORTH, LANCASHIRE

A SEARCH PARTY RETURNS AFTER RETRIEVING
THE BALL AT TILLINGALE, WORCESTERSHIRE

JACK PITTOCK OF LITTLE LOWTON, SOMERSET, HAVING HIS PHOTOGRAPH TAKEN
AFTER YET ANOTHER MATCH-WINNING PERFORMANCE

HEATHCOTE FINDLAY, SLOW LEFT-ARM BOWLER FOR GRIDCOT, YORKSHIRE, WHO WAS ONLY
USED BY HIS CAPTAIN IN THE EARLY EVENING TOWARDS THE END OF THE SEASON

AFTER THE GAME AT LEIGHST

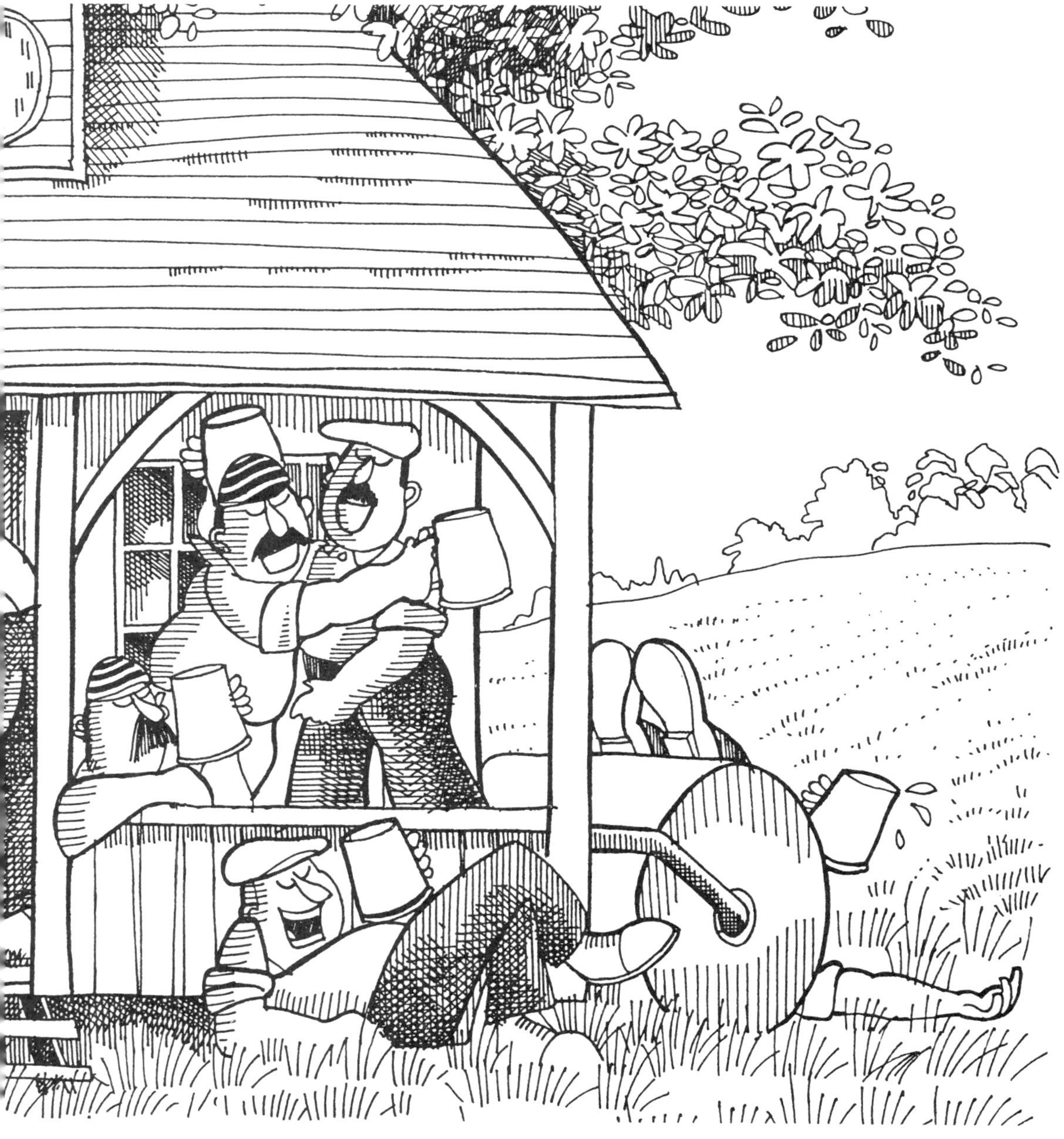

IORY, CORNWALL, 1899

PLAYING FOR A DRAW AT WURBALLBURY, WARWICKSHIRE

PLAYING IN LATE SEPTEMBER AT GREAT TWITE, KENT

REGINALD PILLINGER, THE UMPIRE FOR RAMM END, BEING GIVEN A POLICE ESCORT
AFTER GIVING EIGHT LBW DECISIONS IN THE LOCAL DERBY WITH SAGEMIRE, 1892

OLIVER HOPKIRK RELIVING HIS 3 NOT OUT AFTER THE GAME
AT CHUNDLE COMMON, NORTHUMBERLAND, 1914

MEMBERS OF THE VICTORIOUS TEAM FROM BIDDLETON, YORKSH

EETING A CONSTABLE ON THEIR WAY HOME